America

A Patriotic Primer

America

A Patriotic Primer

Lynne Cheney

Illustrated by

Robin Preiss Glasser

SCHOLASTIC INC.

New York Toronto London Auckland Sydney
Mexico City New Delhi Hong Kong Buenos Aires

ACKNOWLEDGMENTS

My first thanks are to Robin Preiss Glasser, whose imagination and talent have so enriched this book. I would also like to thank Stephanie Lundberg, my intelligent and efficient research assistant, for the help she has given me, and Jacqueline Preiss Weitzman, who has been smart and tireless in unearthing information for Robin.

My colleagues at the American Enterprise Institute warrant special acknowledgment. All of them together create a rich intellectual environment in which all kinds of ideas thrive, even an idea for a children's book. I'd like particularly to recognize Walter Berns for the inspiration he has provided on the subject of patriotism; Robert Goldwin for his profound knowledge, so willingly shared, of the founding period; and Chris DeMuth, president of the American Enterprise Institute, for his constant encouragement.

This book has benefited mightily from Brenda Bowen and Lee Wade, its gifted editor and designer at Simon and Schuster. And last but not least, Robert Barnett, my agent on this book, deserves much thanks for bringing us all together.

—L. C.

ISBN 0-439-45994-X

Book design by Lee Wade
The text for this book is set in Celestia Antique.
The illustrations for this book are rendered in black ink, watercolor washes, and colored pencils.
The author wishes to thank Joe Rosenthal, whose famous photograph of the flag raising at Iwo Jima
was the inspiration for the cover image of America, and for the picture on page 30.
The drawn image of Martha Graham on page 25 is based on Barbara Morgan's copyrighted photo,
Letter to the World (kick), 1940, copyright © Barbara Morgan, Barbara Morgan Archives, and is used by permission.
Mrs. Cheney is donating her net proceeds from this book to the American Red Cross and to projects that foster appreciation of American history.
Editor's Note: Archaic spelling, capitalization, and punctuation in historical quotations have been modernized throughout the text.

To Kate, Elizabeth, and Grace
—L. C.

To my mother, Marcia Preiss,
who continues to inspire me
—R. P. G.

AND TO AMERICA'S CHILDREN

We live in a land of shining cities and natural splendors, a beautiful land made more beautiful still by our commitment to freedom. I wrote this book because I want my grandchildren to understand how blessed we are. I want them to know they are part of a nation whose citizens enjoy liberty and opportunity such as have never been known before. Generations have passed from the earth never dreaming that people could be as fortunate as we Americans are.

I want my granddaughters to know that, and I want them to love this country. Their parents want this for them too, and so what they do, and what the Vice President and I do, is teach them about the United States, about its geography and its people and its history. We believe, all of us, that the story of this country is its highest recommendation. Few tales are more wondrous than that of the founders of this country seeking independence and—against the odds—winning it. Few plots are more thrilling than their deciding to establish a representative form of government and—against the odds—succeeding. And few stories are more heartening than the way that the idea of equality, which was the basis for their actions, has expanded over the subsequent two centuries, including more and ever more of us in the phrase "we the people."

I hope that parents and grandparents will use this book to teach children about Washington's character, Jefferson's intellect, and Madison's wide-ranging knowledge. The upcoming generation should know about these men and their thoughts and aspirations. They should also know about the courage of Frederick Douglass, the determination of Elizabeth Cady Stanton and Susan B. Anthony, and the impassioned leadership of Martin Luther King Jr. Our children should realize that these men and women made us a better country.

We have benefited from the freedom we have enjoyed, and so has all of humankind.

As Abraham Lincoln described it, this realization was one of the reasons that Henry Clay, a luminary of American political life before the Civil War, was so deeply patriotic. Clay "loved his country," Lincoln said, "partly because it was his own country, but mostly because it was a free country; and he burned with a zeal for its advancement, prosperity and glory, because he saw in such, the advancement, prosperity and glory of human liberty, human right and human nature."

Our children should also know that you do not have to be born in this country to be an American. People born elsewhere can become citizens by taking an oath promising that they will be faithful to the Constitution, the plan of government that makes it possible for us to live in freedom. And then when they have taken the oath, they pledge allegiance to the flag and to the republic for which it stands, one nation under God, indivisible, with liberty and justice for all. By committing themselves to our founding principles, people from all around the world become part of "we the people," an equal part because the principles now apply to them.

Mary Antin, who at the end of the nineteenth century came to this country from Russia as a child, described in a book the ongoing amazement she felt at having become an American. One day, she wrote, she learned about George Washington, and suddenly she realized, "I was more nobly related than I had ever supposed. . . . George Washington, who died long before I was born, was like a king in greatness, and he and I were fellow citizens."

Mary Antin's book is called *The Promised Land,* and there are many reasons that so many people from so many countries have looked on the United States in this way. We should all commit ourselves to seeing that the children of this blessed country understand these reasons from their youngest years.

Lynne Cheney

A is for *America*, the land that we love.

"I lift my lamp
beside the golden door!"
—Emma Lazarus

O beautiful for patriot dream that sees beyond the years
Thine alabaster cities gleam undimmed by human tears!

B is for the *Birthday* of this nation of ours.

On America's birthday there ought to be "pomp and parade," John Adams, our second president, wrote to his wife, Abigail, and "illuminations from one end of this continent to the other from this time forward forever more."

C is for the Constitution that binds us together.

The Constitution has been the framework for our government for more than two hundred years.

THE CONSTITUTION, THE DECLARATION OF INDEPENDENCE, AND THE BILL OF RIGHTS ARE KEPT IN THE NATIONAL ARCHIVES BUILDING IN WASHINGTON, D.C., TODAY.

Lincoln Memorial

Washington Monument

White House

National Archives

National Mall

U.S. Supreme Court

U.S. Capitol

Washington, D.C.

Tidal Basin

Jefferson Memorial

"The happy union of these states is a wonder; their constitution a miracle; their example the hope of liberty throughout the world."—James Madison

establish this Constitution for the United States of America.—Preamble to the U.S. Constitution

domestic tranquility, provide for the common defense, promote the general welfare,

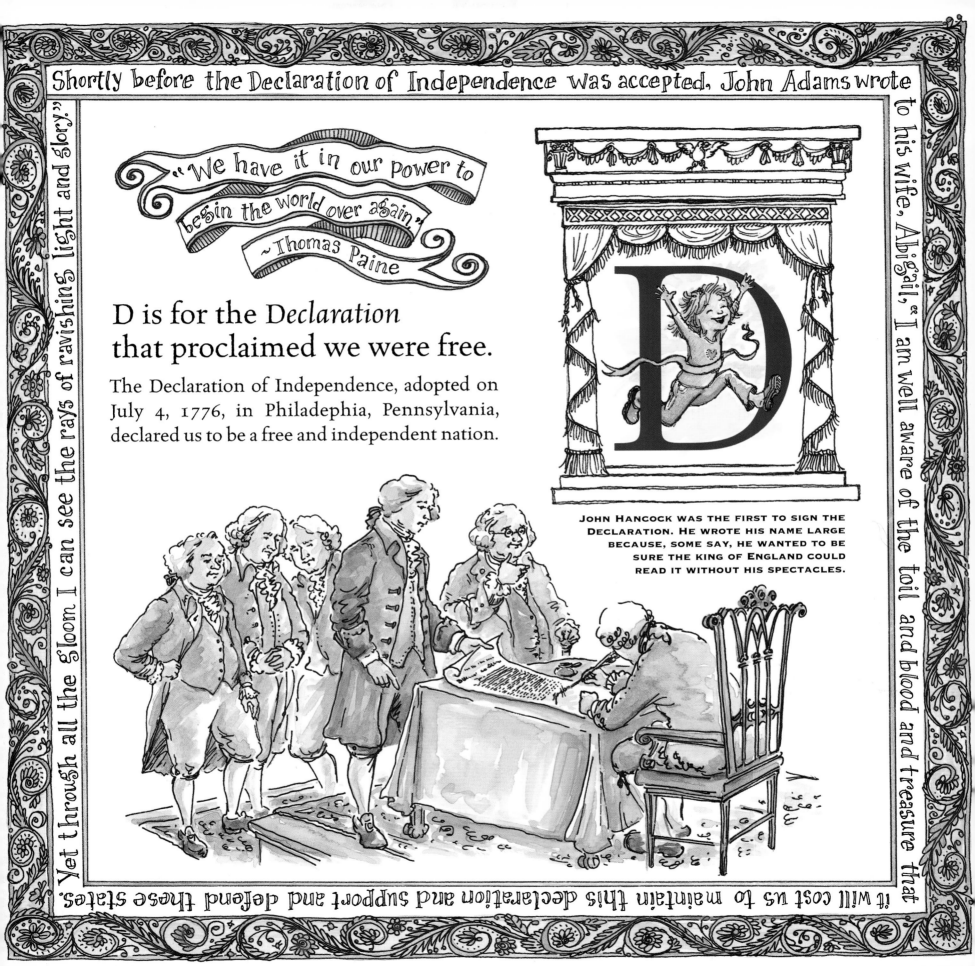

"We have it in our power to begin the world over again."
~Thomas Paine

D is for the *Declaration* that proclaimed we were free.

The Declaration of Independence, adopted on July 4, 1776, in Philadephia, Pennsylvania, declared us to be a free and independent nation.

JOHN HANCOCK WAS THE FIRST TO SIGN THE DECLARATION. HE WROTE HIS NAME LARGE BECAUSE, SOME SAY, HE WANTED TO BE SURE THE KING OF ENGLAND COULD READ IT WITHOUT HIS SPECTACLES.

to his wife, Abigail, "I am well aware of the toil and blood and treasure that

it will cost us to maintain this declaration and defend and support these states.

Yet through all the gloom I can see the rays of ravishing light and glory."

Adopted on June 14, 1777, the first flag of the United States of America had 13 stripes and 13 stars representing the 13 colonies.

Our flag today has 50 stars representing our 50 states and 13 stripes reminding us of the first 13 colonies.

Some vexillologists, or flag experts, believe the first flag was created by Francis Hopkinson.

A huge flag, 30 by 42 feet, was sewn by Mary Pickersgill. It flew over Fort McHenry during the War of 1812 when the British attacked Baltimore.

EQUALITY TIME LINE: **1791 BILL OF RIGHTS.** Guarantees basic rights of citizens.   **1865 AMENDMENT XIII TO U.S. CONSTITUTION.**

1990 AMERICANS WITH DISABILITIES ACT. Prohibits discrimination against people with disabilities.

of African Americans.

E is for *Equality*.

The Declaration of Independence established the principle that all are created equal and have God-given rights to live, to be free, and to pursue happiness. Over the years, more and more of us have been able to enjoy these rights equally.

ston Elementary School

office

1965 VOTING RIGHTS ACT. Strikes down restrictions used to deny the voting rights

discrimination on basis of "race, color, religion, sex, or national origin."

Francis Scott Key wrote the words to our national anthem, "The Star-Spangled Banner," when he saw this flag still waving after the attack.

How to fold a flag

Step 1

Francis Bellamy is credited with writing the Pledge of Allegiance in Boston, 1892.

When the flag passes by in a parade, all persons should salute.

"The Stars and Stripes Forever," our national march, was first performed in 1897.

F is for Freedom and the Flag that we fly.

"I pledge allegiance to the flag of the United States of America and to the Republic for which it stands, one nation under God, indivisible, with liberty and justice for all."

Flag flown upside down indicates distress or S.O.S.

Flag flown at half-staff indicates mourning.

1934 INDIAN REORGANIZATION ACT. Protects land holdings of Native American reservations.

1948 EXECUTIVE ORDER 9981. Ends segregation in U.S. military.

1954 BROWN V. BOARD OF EDUCATION. Makes school segregation unconstitutional.

1964 CIVIL RIGHTS ACT. Prohibits

Flag should be carried properly folded.

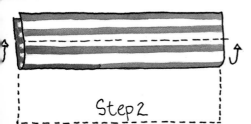
Step 2

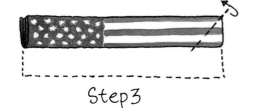
Step 3

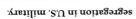

Step 4

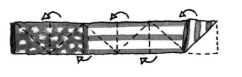

G is for *God* in whom we trust.

Freedom to worship as they chose brought people to America. Freedom to worship as we choose sustains our country today.

IN 1620 THE PILGRIMS SAILED TO AMERICA IN SEARCH OF FREEDOM TO WORSHIP GOD IN THEIR OWN WAY. AFTER THEY HAD CROSSED THE VAST AND STORMY OCEAN, THEY DREW UP A PLAN FOR GOVERNING THEMSELVES CALLED THE MAYFLOWER COMPACT.

THE PILGRIMS' FIRST WINTER WAS VERY HARD, BUT IN THE SPRING, NATIVE AMERICANS OF THE WAMPANOAG TRIBE TAUGHT THEM HOW TO GROW CORN AND CATCH FISH. AFTER A SUCCESSFUL HARVEST, THE PILGRIMS INVITED THE WAMPANOAG TO JOIN IN A FEAST. TODAY WE THINK OF THEIR CELEBRATION AS THE FIRST THANKSGIVING.

H is for *Heroes* and I for *Ideals*.
Heroes remind us of our nation's ideals and how important it is to live up to them.

PIONEERS

FIREFIGHTERS

U.S. MILITARY

Some heroes we admire from afar.
Others are part of our lives every day.

ASTRONAUTS

DOCTORS AND NURSES

POLICE

TEACHERS

ELECTED LEADERS

"The God who gave us life gave us liberty at the same time." —Thomas Jefferson

"The last hope of human liberty in this world rests on us." said Jefferson in 1811.

THE VIRGINIA STATUTE FOR RELIGIOUS FREEDOM, WRITTEN BY JEFFERSON, WAS A FORERUNNER OF THE FIRST AMENDMENT.

Louisiana Purchase 1803

existing states

New Spain

WITH THE LOUISIANA PURCHASE, PRESIDENT JEFFERSON DOUBLED THE SIZE OF THE UNITED STATES. IT WAS A BARGAIN AT LESS THAN THREE CENTS AN ACRE.

THE UNIVERSITY OF VIRGINIA, DESIGNED BY JEFFERSON, WAS ONE OF HIS PROUDEST ACCOMPLISHMENTS.

J is for *Jefferson*.

In 1776 Thomas Jefferson wrote the Declaration of Independence. He was the first secretary of state, the second vice president, and our third president.

JEFFERSON'S HOME WAS MONTICELLO, WHICH HE DESIGNED AND LIVED IN MOST OF HIS LIFE.

"I cannot live without books."

JEFFERSON INVENTED MANY THINGS, INCLUDING A PLOW AND THIS COPYING MACHINE.

We hold these truths to be self-evident, that all men are created equal, that they are endowed by their creator with certain inalienable rights; that are life, liberty, & the pursuit of happiness; that to secure these rights, governments are instituted among men, deriving their just powers from the consent of the governed; that whenever any form of government becomes destructive of these ends, it is the right of the people to alter or to abolish it, & to institute new government, laying its foundation on such principles...

♪ Oh, deep in my heart, I do believe we shall overcome someday. ♪

THOUSANDS OF PEOPLE LED BY DR. KING MARCHED FROM SELMA TO MONTGOMERY, ALABAMA, IN MARCH 1965. THEY HELPED CONVINCE CONGRESS TO PASS A LAW ENSURING THAT AFRICAN AMERICANS COULD VOTE.

K is for King.

Dr. Martin Luther King Jr. fought for justice with prayers, peaceful marches, and some of the most powerful words our nation has ever heard.

"I have a dream that my four children will one day live in a nation where they will not be judged by the color of their skin but by the content of their character."

"Let justice roll down like waters."

AFTER BEING JAILED FOR A PEACEFUL PROTEST, DR. KING WROTE "LETTER FROM BIRMINGHAM JAIL," IN WHICH HE DECLARED, "INJUSTICE ANYWHERE IS A THREAT TO JUSTICE EVERYWHERE."

BECAUSE HE FOUGHT VIOLENCE WITH PEACEFUL PROTEST, DR. KING WAS AWARDED THE NOBEL PEACE PRIZE. HE WAS ONLY THIRTY-FIVE YEARS OLD.

LINCOLN, BORN IN A LOG CABIN, GREW UP TO BE KNOWN AS HONEST ABE.

LINCOLN'S CHILDREN TAD AND WILLIE WERE THE FIRST PRESIDENTIAL CHILDREN TO LIVE IN THE WHITE HOUSE.

"I happen temporarily to occupy this big White House. I am a living witness that any one of your children may look to come here as my father's child has."

WHEN LINCOLN WAS ELECTED PRESIDENT, SOUTHERN STATES LEFT THE UNION, AND THE CIVIL WAR BROKE OUT.

L is for Lincoln.

Abraham Lincoln, our sixteenth president, guided our nation during the Civil War. He was determined that we would continue to be a single nation.

IN 1863 LINCOLN ISSUED THE EMANCIPATION PROCLAMATION FREEING ENSLAVED AFRICAN AMERICANS IN THE CONFEDERACY.

THE UNION WON THE WAR, BUT ON APRIL 14, 1865, LINCOLN WAS KILLED. A FUNERAL TRAIN TOOK HIM HOME TO ILLINOIS. AMERICANS WILL REMEMBER HIM ALWAYS AS A GREAT MAN AND A GREAT PRESIDENT.

JAMES MADISON'S WIFE, DOLLEY, WAS GRACIOUS AND BRAVE. DURING THE WAR OF 1812, SHE GATHERED UP IMPORTANT DOCUMENTS AND A PAINTING OF GEORGE WASHINGTON BEFORE SHE FLED THE ADVANCING BRITISH, WHO SET FIRE TO THE WHITE HOUSE.

"The advice nearest to my heart . . . is that the union of the states be cherished and perpetuated."

MADISON STUDIED GOVERNMENTS OF OTHER TIMES AND PLACES TO GET IDEAS ABOUT HOW OUR OWN SHOULD BE FORMED.

M is for *Madison*.

James Madison, our fourth president, was so important when our nation was getting started that he is called the Father of the Constitution. He was primarily responsible for the Bill of Rights.

MADISON WAS ONE OF THE AUTHORS OF THE FEDERALIST PAPERS, ESSAYS THAT HELPED CONVINCE THE STATES TO ACCEPT THE CONSTITUTION.

IN THE STREETS OUTSIDE INDEPENDENCE HALL, PHILADELPHIANS WAITED IN THE SUMMER OF 1787 TO SEE WHAT KIND OF GOVERNMENT MADISON AND THE OTHER DELEGATES HAD DECIDED ON. "WHAT HAVE WE GOT?" A WOMAN ASKED BEN FRANKLIN. "A REPUBLIC," HE REPLIED, "IF YOU CAN KEEP IT."

We the People...

Amendments

The U.S. Constitution

The U.S. Bill of Rights

POCAHONTAS, DAUGHTER OF POWHATAN, HELPED THE COLONISTS AT JAMESTOWN.

TECUMSEH, A SHAWNEE LEADER, WITH HIS BROTHER, THE PROPHET, ORGANIZED NATIVE AMERICAN NATIONS INTO A CONFEDERATION.

SEQUOYAH, A CHEROKEE, CREATED AN ALPHABET FOR HIS PEOPLE.

JIM THORPE, OF SAC AND FOX HERITAGE, WAS ONE OF THE GREATEST ATHLETES OF THE TWENTIETH CENTURY.

N is for Native Americans, who came here first.

SACAJAWEA, A SHOSHONE WOMAN, GUIDED AND TRANSLATED FOR LEWIS AND CLARK AS THEY EXPLORED THE WEST.

NAVAJO CODE TALKERS, WORLD WAR II MARINES, USED THEIR NATIVE LANGUAGE TO SEND CODED MESSAGES. THE JAPANESE NEVER DECIPHERED THEIR TRANSMISSIONS.

MARIA TALLCHIEF OF THE OSAGE TRIBE BECAME A PRIMA BALLERINA.

BEN NIGHTHORSE CAMPBELL, ONE OF FORTY-FOUR CHIEFS OF THE NORTHERN CHEYENNE TRIBE, IS A U.S. SENATOR FROM COLORADO.

ACCORDING TO ONE ESTIMATE, MORE THAN 40 PERCENT OF AMERICANS LIVING TODAY HAVE AN ANCESTOR WHO PASSED THROUGH ELLIS ISLAND, THE ENTRY POINT TO AMERICA FOR MILLIONS OF IMMIGRANTS.

"I hereby declare, on oath, . . . that I will support and defend the Constitution and laws of the United States of America."
—from the Oath of Citizenship

O is for the *Oath* new Americans take.

"Our obligations to our country never cease but with our lives." John Adams

P is for the *Patriotism* that fills our hearts with pride.

Lemonade 25¢ for Red Cross

Louis Armstrong: jazz trumpeter, singer, and bandleader

Emily Dickinson: groundbreaking poet

Babe Ruth: baseball legend

Althea Gibson: tennis champion

Orville and Wilbur Wright: first successful powered flight

Martha Graham: modern-dance innovator

I. M. Pei: world-renowned architect

Q is for America's Quest for the new, the far, and the very best.

Thomas Edison: inventor of the light-bulb, motion-picture projector, and phonograph

Benjamin Franklin: inventor, scientist, statesman

"We choose to go to the moon . . . and do the other things, not because they are easy, but because they are hard, because that goal will serve to organize and measure the best of our energies and skills."—John F. Kennedy

FREEDOM OF SPEECH

FREEDOM OF THE PRESS

FREEDOM OF RELIGION

FREEDOM OF ASSEMBLY

R is for the *Rights* we are guaranteed.

Our basic rights are set forth in the Constitution and its amendments. The first ten amendments are called the Bill of Rights.

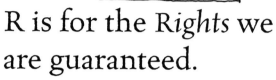

RIGHT TO KEEP AND BEAR ARMS

RIGHT TO TRIAL BY JURY

RIGHT TO VOTE

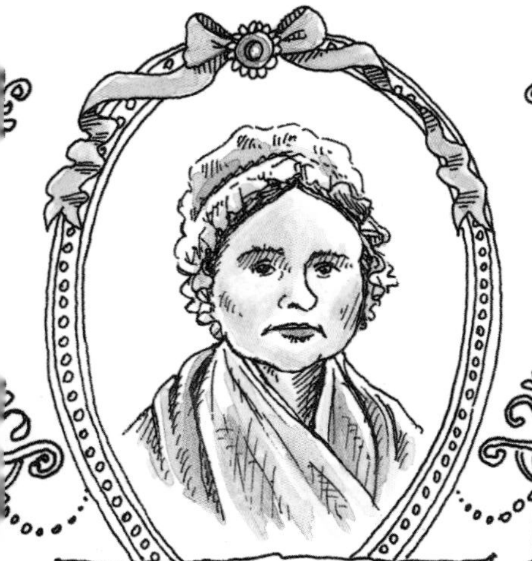

LUCRETIA MOTT

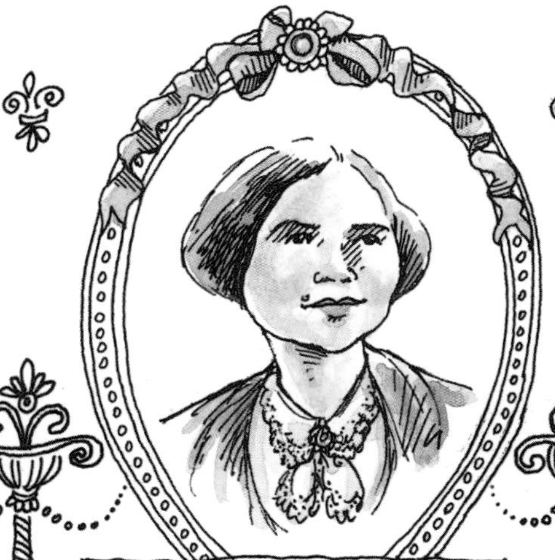

LUCY STONE

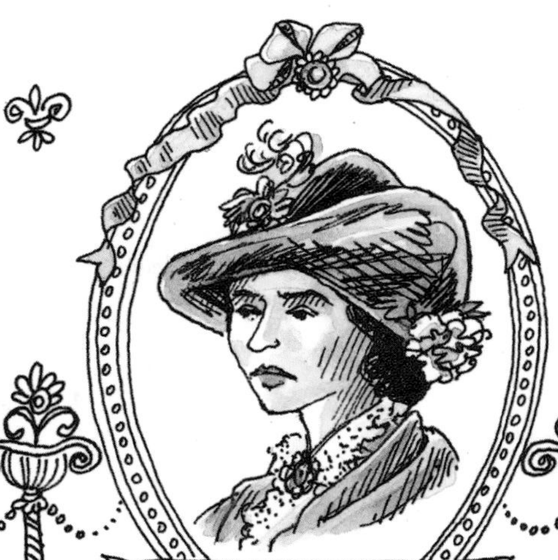

ALICE PAUL

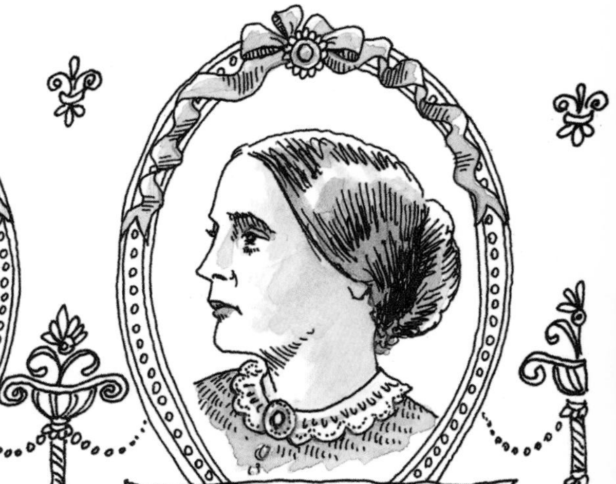

SUSAN B. ANTHONY

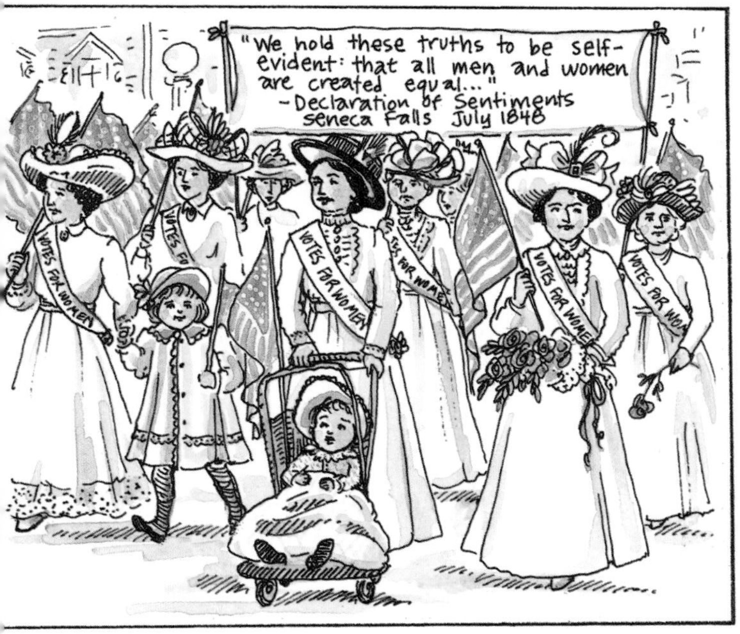

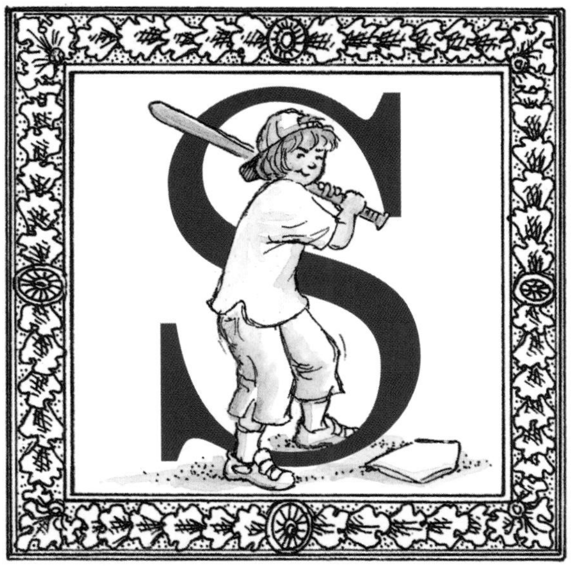

"We hold these truths to be self-evident: that all men and women are created equal..."
—Declaration of Sentiments
Seneca Falls July 1848

VOTES FOR WOMEN

S is for *Suffrage*.

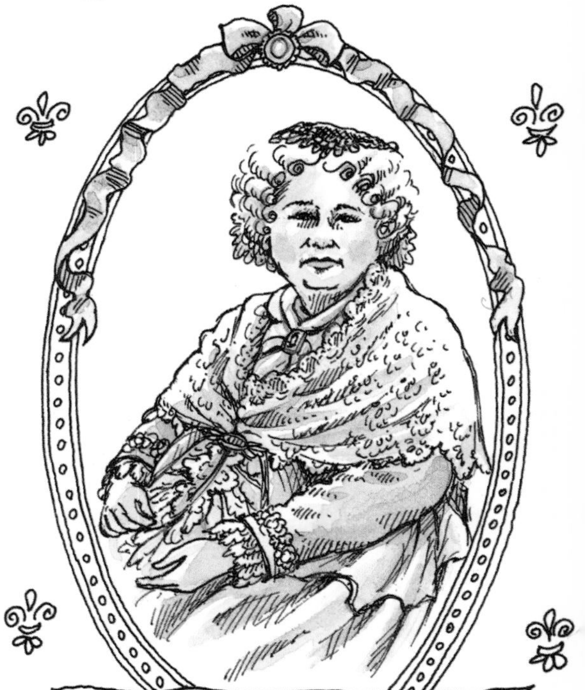

ELIZABETH CADY STANTON

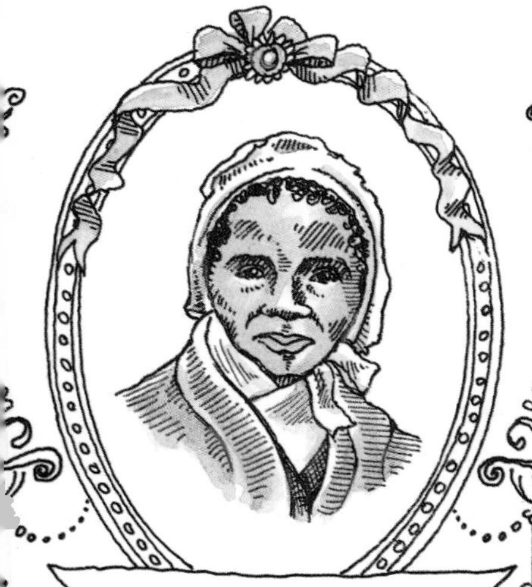

In 1848 in Seneca Falls, New York, women began the long struggle for suffrage, or the right to vote. In 1920 their voting rights were recognized all across the nation.

SOJOURNER TRUTH

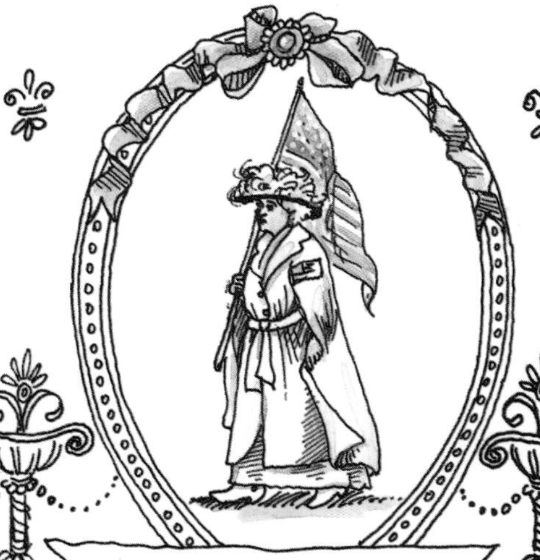

CARRIE CHAPMAN CATT

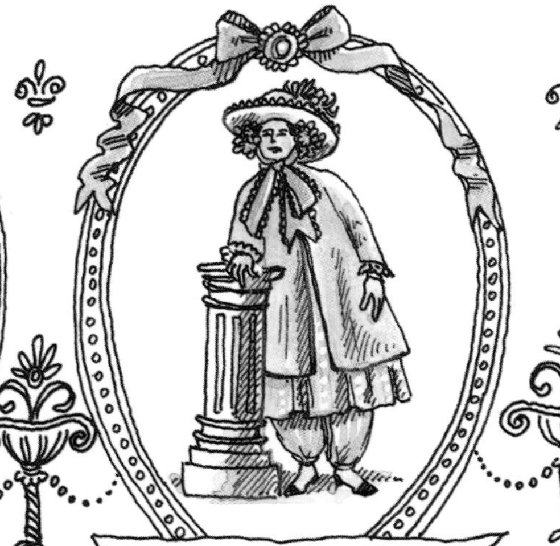

AMELIA BLOOMER

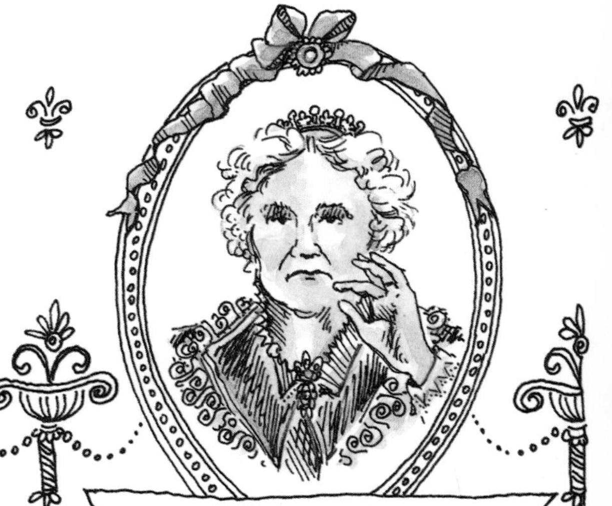

ESTHER HOBART MORRIS

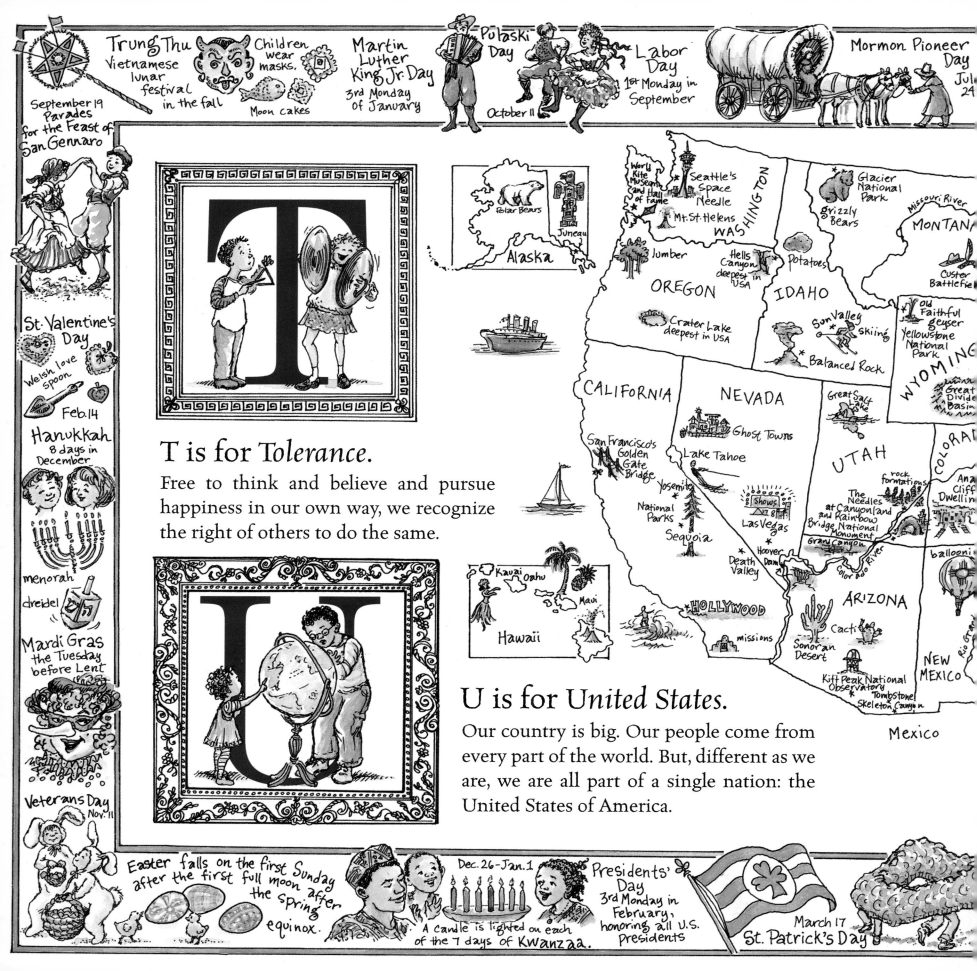

Trung Thu — Vietnamese lunar festival in the fall. September 19. Children wear masks. Moon cakes.

Parades for the Feast of San Gennaro

Martin Luther King Jr. Day — 3rd Monday of January

Pulaski Day — October 11

Labor Day — 1st Monday in September

Mormon Pioneer Day — July 24

St. Valentine's Day — Feb. 14 — Welsh love spoon

Hanukkah — 8 days in December — menorah — dreidel

Mardi Gras — the Tuesday before Lent

Veterans Day — Nov. 11

T is for *Tolerance*.

Free to think and believe and pursue happiness in our own way, we recognize the right of others to do the same.

U is for *United States*.

Our country is big. Our people come from every part of the world. But, different as we are, we are all part of a single nation: the United States of America.

Alaska — Polar Bears — Juneau

Hawaii — Kauai, Oahu, Maui

WASHINGTON — Seattle's Space Needle — World Kite Museum and Hall of Fame — Mt. St. Helens

OREGON — Lumber — Crater Lake deepest in USA

IDAHO — Hells Canyon deepest in USA — Potatoes — Sun Valley — skiing — Balanced Rock

MONTANA — Grizzly Bears — Missouri River — Custer Battlefield — Glacier National Park

WYOMING — Old Faithful geyser — Yellowstone National Park — Great Divide Basin

CALIFORNIA — San Francisco's Golden Gate Bridge — Yosemite — National Parks — Sequoia — Death Valley — Hollywood — missions

NEVADA — Ghost Towns — Lake Tahoe — Shows — Las Vegas — Hoover Dam

UTAH — Great Salt Lake — The Needles at Canyonland and Rainbow Bridge National Monument — rock formations

COLORADO — Anasazi Cliff Dwellings — Grand Canyon — Colorado River — ballooning

ARIZONA — Cacti — Sonoran Desert — Kitt Peak National Observatory — Tombstone — Skeleton Canyon

NEW MEXICO — Rio Grande

Mexico

Easter falls on the first Sunday after the first full moon after the spring equinox.

Dec. 26–Jan. 1 — A candle is lighted on each of the 7 days of Kwanzaa.

Presidents' Day — 3rd Monday in February, honoring all U.S. Presidents

March 17 — St. Patrick's Day

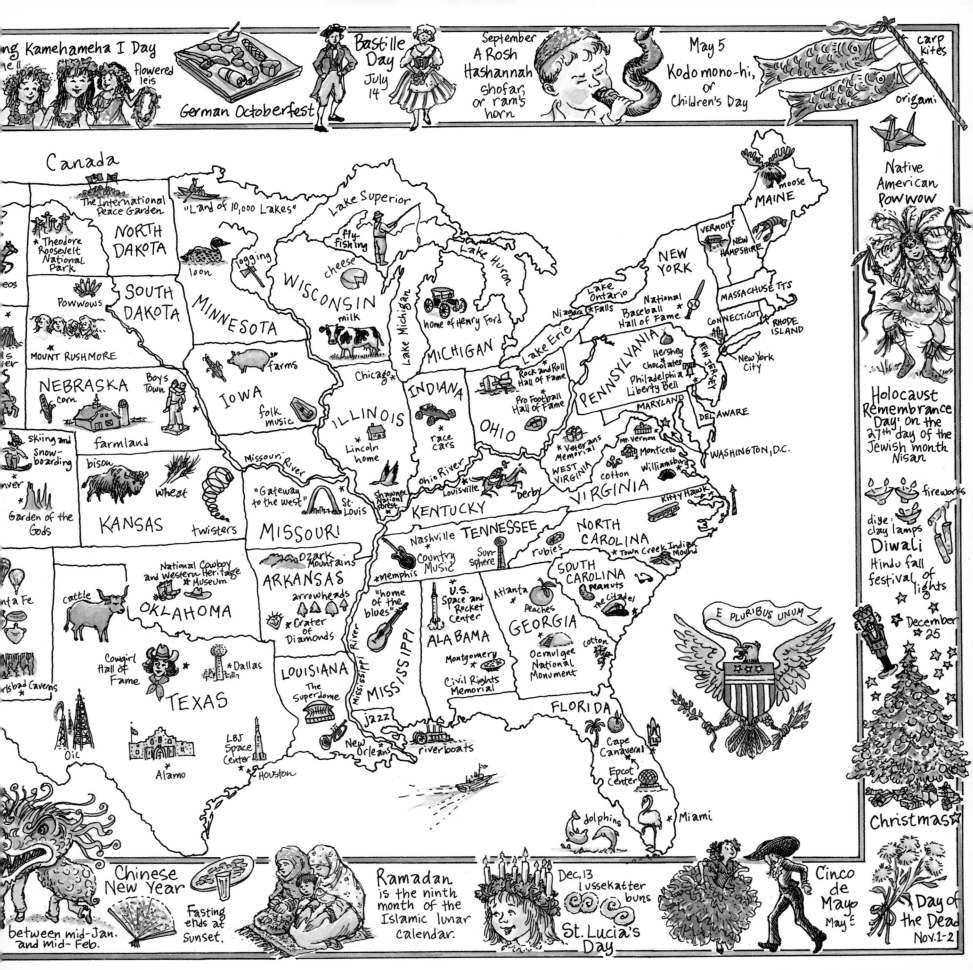

Navy Cross

Silver Star

MOLLY PITCHER: ONE OF THE FIRST AMERICAN WOMEN TO FIGHT FOR FREEDOM.

COURAGEOUS WORLD WAR II MARINES HELPED WIN THE WAR IN THE PACIFIC.

V is for the *Valor* shown by those who've kept us free.

IN WORLD WAR II, BRAVE PARATROOPERS PARACHUTED BEHIND ENEMY LINES.

54TH MASSACHUSETTS REGIMENT: AN AFRICAN-AMERICAN UNIT THAT FOUGHT WITH GREAT VALOR IN THE CIVIL WAR.

442ND REGIMENTAL COMBAT TEAM: A JAPANESE-AMERICAN UNIT THAT BECAME ONE OF THE MOST DECORATED IN MILITARY HISTORY.

AMERICAN SAILORS WON THE BATTLE OF MIDWAY AND TURNED THE COURSE OF WORLD WAR II.

ALVIN C. YORK: WORLD WAR I

Medal of Honor

AUDIE MURPHY: WORLD WAR II

BRAVE AMERICAN SOLDIERS FOUGHT IN THE JUNGLES OF VIETNAM.

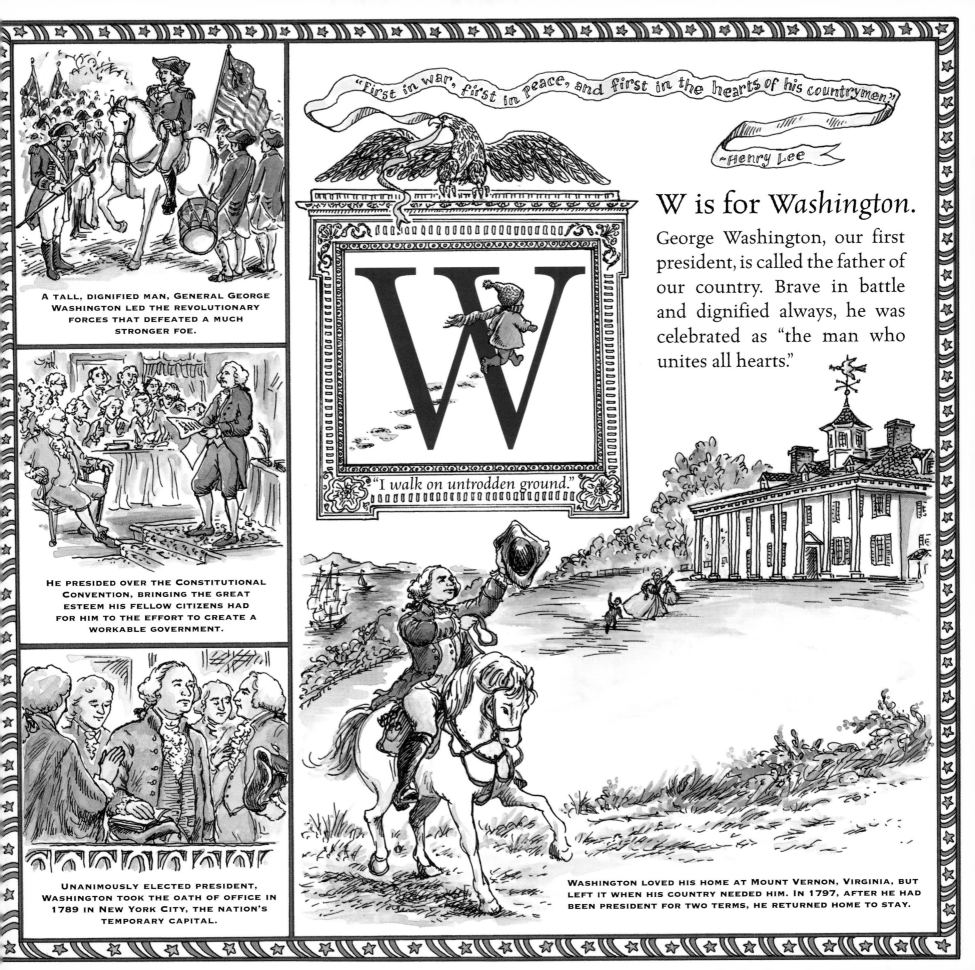

A TALL, DIGNIFIED MAN, GENERAL GEORGE WASHINGTON LED THE REVOLUTIONARY FORCES THAT DEFEATED A MUCH STRONGER FOE.

HE PRESIDED OVER THE CONSTITUTIONAL CONVENTION, BRINGING THE GREAT ESTEEM HIS FELLOW CITIZENS HAD FOR HIM TO THE EFFORT TO CREATE A WORKABLE GOVERNMENT.

UNANIMOUSLY ELECTED PRESIDENT, WASHINGTON TOOK THE OATH OF OFFICE IN 1789 IN NEW YORK CITY, THE NATION'S TEMPORARY CAPITAL.

"First in war, first in peace, and first in the hearts of his countrymen."

~Henry Lee

"I walk on untrodden ground."

W is for Washington.

George Washington, our first president, is called the father of our country. Brave in battle and dignified always, he was celebrated as "the man who unites all hearts."

WASHINGTON LOVED HIS HOME AT MOUNT VERNON, VIRGINIA, BUT LEFT IT WHEN HIS COUNTRY NEEDED HIM. IN 1797, AFTER HE HAD BEEN PRESIDENT FOR TWO TERMS, HE RETURNED HOME TO STAY.

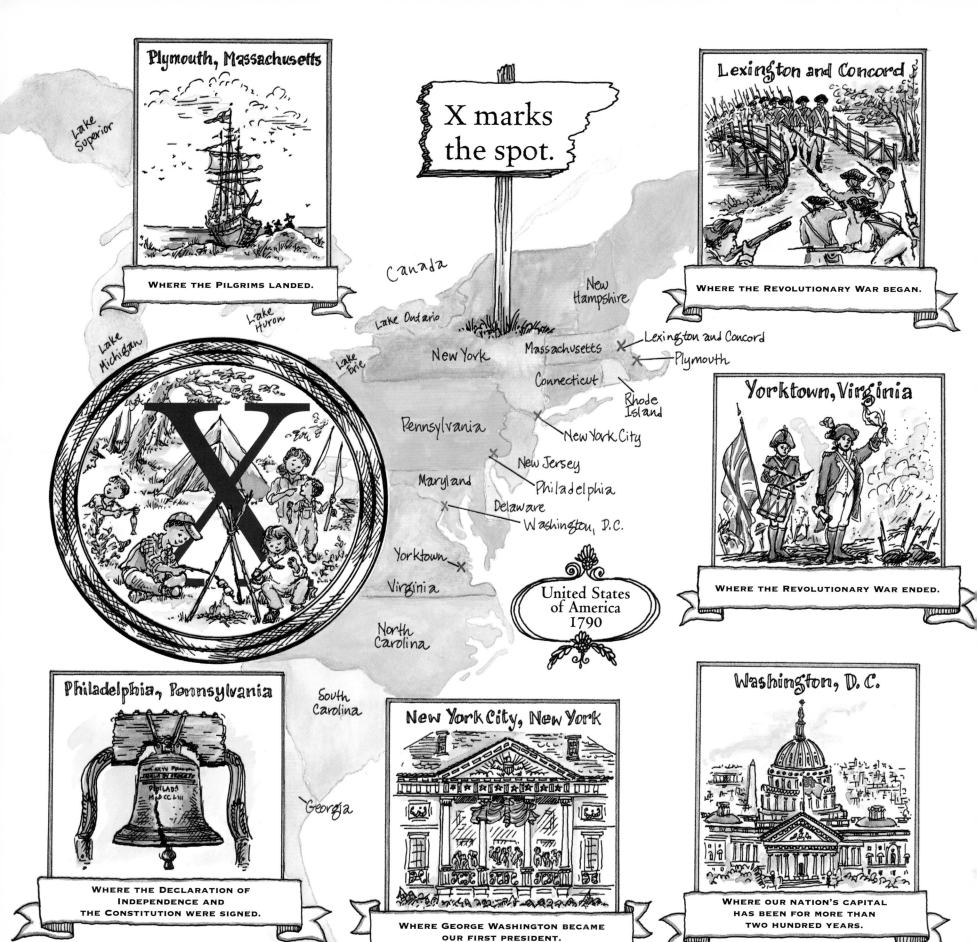

Plymouth, Massachusetts

WHERE THE PILGRIMS LANDED.

X marks the spot.

Lexington and Concord

WHERE THE REVOLUTIONARY WAR BEGAN.

Lake Superior

Lake Huron

Lake Michigan

Lake Erie

Lake Ontario

Canada

New Hampshire

New York

Massachusetts — Lexington and Concord

— Plymouth

Connecticut

Rhode Island

Pennsylvania

New York City

New Jersey

Philadelphia

Maryland

Delaware

Washington, D.C.

Yorktown

Virginia

North Carolina

United States of America 1790

South Carolina

Georgia

Yorktown, Virginia

WHERE THE REVOLUTIONARY WAR ENDED.

Philadelphia, Pennsylvania

WHERE THE DECLARATION OF INDEPENDENCE AND THE CONSTITUTION WERE SIGNED.

New York City, New York

WHERE GEORGE WASHINGTON BECAME OUR FIRST PRESIDENT.

Washington, D.C.

WHERE OUR NATION'S CAPITAL HAS BEEN FOR MORE THAN TWO HUNDRED YEARS.

Y is for *You* and all you will be in this greatest of countries, the land of the free.

"The noblest question in the world is: What good may I do in it?"
—Benjamin Franklin

Z is the end of the alphabet, but not of America's story. Strong and free, we will continue to be an inspiration to the world.

"*I know that for America there will always be a bright dawn ahead.*"—Ronald Reagan

America! America! God shed his grace on thee and crown thy good with brotherhood from sea to shining sea!

NOTES ON THE TEXT

I wrote this book so that children could enjoy it by themselves, but I like to think that it will most often be read and discussed by parents and children together. Those who wish to continue the discussion beyond the page devoted to each letter of the alphabet should find the following explanatory material of use.—L. C.

A

A portion of Emma Lazarus's 1883 poem "The New Colossus" is inscribed on the Statue of Liberty: "Give me your tired, your poor, / Your huddled masses yearning to breathe free, / The wretched refuse of your teeming shore. / Send these, the homeless, tempest-tossed to me: / I lift my lamp beside the golden door!"

Katharine Lee Bates, who taught at Wellesley College, wrote "America the Beautiful" in 1893. The beginning of the last stanza is quoted in the banner at the bottom of the page.

B

John Adams, who wrote about "pomp and parade" on July 3, 1776, thought that America's birthday would be celebrated on July 2, the day the Continental Congress voted that the colonies were free and independent states. But Americans have long celebrated instead on July 4, the day the Congress formally approved the Declaration of Independence.

C

Signed in Philadelphia on September 17, 1787, the Constitution had to be ratified, or accepted, by nine of the thirteen original states. That threshold was met in June 1788, when New Hampshire became the ninth state to ratify. Now the oldest enduring written national constitution, the U.S. Constitution has served as a model for others around the world.

James Madison wrote about the "miracle" of the Constitution in 1829.

The Declaration of Independence, the Constitution, and the Bill of Rights, usually on public display at the National Archives, will be available for public viewing again in 2003 when renovation of the rotunda and exhibit halls is completed.

The Constitution provides for three branches of government: the executive (symbolized by the White House, where the president lives and works), the legislative (by the Capitol, where Congress meets), and the judicial (by the Supreme Court Building, where the nine justices meet and deliberate).

D

The Tom Paine quotation is from *Common Sense,* a pamphlet published in January 1776 that helped convince Americans it was time to seek independence from England.

John Adams wrote about the difficulties that would follow the American colonists' decision to seek independence in a letter to his wife, Abigail, on July 3, 1776.

On July 4, John Hancock, as president of the Congress, signed the Declaration, and Charles Thomson, secretary of the Congress, certi-

fied it. The document was then transferred to parchment, and eventually fifty-six delegates signed, pledging lives, fortunes, and "sacred honor" to the cause of independence.

E and F

Even after the Indian Citizenship Act, some states did not allow Native Americans to vote. It took until 1962, but finally all fifty states recognized Native American voting rights.

When the flag passes in review, persons in uniform render the military salute. Those not in uniform stand at attention and place the right hand over the heart. The same etiquette applies during the pledge of allegiance and the playing of the national anthem.

Mary Pickersgill was assisted in making the flag for Fort McHenry by her thirteen-year-old daughter, Caroline. Mrs. Pickersgill was paid $405.90 for making the flag.

John Philip Sousa composed "The Stars and Stripes Forever."

G

The Mayflower Compact, a landmark document in the history of self-government, was named after the Pilgrims' small ship, the *Mayflower.*

Squanto, or Tisquantum, who spoke English, was the Native American who helped the Pilgrims the most. He had been kidnapped, sold into slavery in Spain, and had escaped to England. He had made his way back to America not long before the Pilgrims arrived. They called him "a special instrument sent of God."

H and I

Eleanor Roosevelt (1884–1962): Wife of President Franklin D. Roosevelt, she worked to help the less fortunate and to advance the cause of women.

John Adams (1735–1826): A prime mover in the drive for American independence, Adams became the first vice president of the United States and its second president.

Abigail Adams (1744–1818): Wife of John Adams, she was a woman of great strength and wisdom. John and Abigail's son, John Quincy Adams, became the sixth president of the United States.

Franklin D. Roosevelt (1882–1945): America's thirty-second president, he was a resolute leader during two of the nation's darkest times, the Great Depression and World War II.

Sam Houston (1793–1863): He led the Texas army in the successful fight for independence from Mexico, served as president of the independent Republic of Texas, and, after Texas was admitted to the Union, as a senator and governor. When he stood firm against the wish of Texas voters to leave the Union, he was deposed from office.

Harriet Tubman (1820?–1913): She escaped slavery by fleeing to the North and then repeatedly risked her freedom and her life by returning to the South to help hundreds of others escape.

Chief Joseph (1840?–1904): After fighting broke out between the Nez Perce and the U.S. Army, this brave chief led his people on a 1,400-mile march with the goal of finding refuge in Canada. Forced to surrender before he reached the border, he said, "My heart is sick and sad. From where the sun now stands, I will fight no more forever."

Jackie Robinson (1919–1972): In 1947 he became the first African-American to play modern-day major league baseball. Enduring insult and abuse, he helped his Brooklyn Dodger teammates win the National League pennant and was named rookie of the year. In 1962 he was inducted into the National Baseball Hall of Fame.

Clara Barton (1821–1912): After working as a volunteer distributing supplies and aid to wounded soldiers during the Civil War, this humanitarian (known as the "Angel of the Battlefield") founded the American Red Cross and served as its first president.

Nathan Hale (1755–1776): Captured by the British during the Revolutionary War, Hale, a Connecticut officer, was sentenced to death. He is reported to have said, "I only regret that I have but one life to lose for my country."

Jane Addams (1860–1935): A pioneer social worker, she dedicated her life to the poor. When she founded Hull House, a place where poor people in Chicago could find help, she began a nationwide movement to improve the lives of the less fortunate.

Frederick Douglass (1817–1895): Born in slavery, Douglass taught himself how to write and speak persuasively. After escaping to the North, he used his powerful intellect and noted oratorical skills to seek justice for African-Americans. His autobiography, *Narrative of the Life of Frederick Douglass,* is a literary classic.

Mount Rushmore is located in the Black Hills of South Dakota. Designed by Gutzon Borglum and completed in 1941, it presents heroic sculptures of George Washington, Thomas Jefferson, Theodore Roosevelt, and Abraham Lincoln. Roosevelt, a dedicated outdoorsman, was our twenty-sixth president and a passionate advocate of preserving our nation's natural resources.

Sitting Bull (1831?–1890): A powerful religious and political leader, Sitting Bull, a Sioux chief, organized the Indians who defeated George Armstrong Custer at the Battle of the Little Bighorn in 1876. His grave and memorial, near Mobridge, South Dakota, overlook the Missouri River.

The Tomb of the Unknowns at Arlington National Cemetery in Arlington, Virginia, commemorates the unidentified dead of four wars. The inscription reads: "Here rests in honored glory an American soldier known but to God."

The Portrait Monument to Lucretia Mott, Elizabeth Cady Stanton, and Susan B. Anthony, three leaders of the woman suffrage movement, is in the rotunda of the U.S. Capitol. It was sculpted by Adelaide Johnson in 1920.

The Alamo, located in San Antonio, Texas, is the site of a crucial battle in Texas's war for independence from Mexico. Although overwhelmingly outnumbered by General Santa Anna's army, the defenders of the Alamo held out for thirteen days in 1836. Their brave stand led to the battle cry, "Remember the Alamo!"

The Civil Rights Memorial in Montgomery, Alabama, provides a time line of events and honors those who gave their lives during the civil rights movement. It was dedicated in 1989.

The Vietnam Veterans Memorial commemorates the more than 58,000 Americans who died in the Vietnam War. Of all the memorials in Washington, D.C., this is the one most often visited.

J

In 1774 Jefferson wrote about God's gifts of life and liberty; in 1776 he wrote the Declaration of Independence; in 1787 he encouraged his daughter Martha "never to be idle."

Elected in 1800, Jefferson was the first president to be inaugurated in the nation's new capital, Washington, D.C. Jefferson served until 1809.

In 1811 he wrote about the last hope of human liberty in a letter to newspaper editor William Duane; in 1815 he told John Adams that he could not "live without books."

Jefferson was eighty-three when he died on July 4, 1826. John Adams also died on that day. He was ninety years old. Said Daniel Webster of the two men, "Their work doth not perish with them."

The Virginia Statute for Religious Freedom, which became law in 1786, provided for the separation of church and state.

The Louisiana Purchase, out of which thirteen states and parts of states would be formed, occurred in 1803, when the United States purchased the land from France.

The University of Virginia was founded in 1819. A select number of students today have the honor of living in "Lawn rooms" that Jefferson designed.

Thomas Jefferson loved mockingbirds. Two of them are holding the garland above the letter J.

K

Dr. King was born in Atlanta, Georgia, in 1929. He wrote "Letter from Birmingham Jail" in 1963, the same year he delivered his famed "I have a dream" speech in Washington, D.C. He won the Nobel Peace Prize in 1964.

A minister with a Ph.D. in theology, Dr. King frequently quoted scripture. "Let justice roll down like waters," which he quoted in "Letter from Birmingham Jail," is from the Old Testament book of Amos 5:24.

Dr. King was thirty-nine years old when he was assassinated in Memphis, Tennessee, in 1968.

L

Lincoln was born in 1809 in a log cabin in Kentucky. He moved to Illinois as a young man.

Lincoln made his remarks about children to the 166th Ohio Regiment in 1864.

Lincoln had four sons. The first, Edward, died in 1850. Robert was a university student when his father was elected so only Tad and Willie lived in the White House. Willie died while his father was president.

Lincoln was elected president in 1860. The Civil War began in 1861 and ended in 1865. Lincoln was assassinated at Ford's Theater in Washington, D.C., on April 14, 1865, less than a week after General Robert E. Lee surrendered at Appomattox Court House in Virginia.

M

Madison was born in Virginia in 1751.

His most intensive study of other governments occurred before the Constitutional Convention (1787), when he read dozens upon dozens of books that Thomas Jefferson, at Madison's request, sent from Paris, where Jefferson was representing the United States.

The other authors of the Federalist Papers were Alexander Hamilton and John Jay.

Madison was president from 1809 to 1817. He wrote about "liberty and learning" in 1822.

"The advice nearest my heart" quotation is from a note opened after Madison's death in 1836.

The exchange between the Philadelphia woman and Benjamin Franklin was recorded by Maryland delegate James McHenry.

N

Early migrants to North America began to come across the Bering land bridge from Asia at least 15,000 years ago. In recent years, some investigators have suggested much earlier arrivals, perhaps even by boat.

The tribes named in the border of this page symbolize the diversity of Native American life. There are hundreds of native groups in North America with different customs and cultural heritages.

O

The full text of the Oath of Allegiance, also known as the Oath of Citizenship: "I hearby declare, on oath, that I absolutely and entirely renounce and abjure all allegiance and fidelity to any foreign prince, potentate, state, or sovereignty of whom or which I have heretofore been a subject or citizen; that I will support and defend the Constitution and laws of the United States of America against all enemies, foreign and domestic; that I will bear true faith and allegiance to the same; that I will bear arms on behalf of the United States when required by the law; that I will perform noncombatant service in the Armed Forces of the United States when required by the law; that I will perform work of national importance under civilian direction when required by the law; and that I take this obligation freely without any mental reservation or purpose of evasion; so help me God."

P

John Adams wrote about our obligations to our country in a letter to physician Benjamin Rush in 1808.

Q

The names in the border symbolize thousands upon thousands of Americans whose achievements reflect excellence. Children should be encouraged to add to this list.

Jonas Salk (1914–1995): A physician and scientist, he developed the first polio vaccine.

Babe Didrikson Zaharias (1913–1956): An Olympic track-and-field athlete and champion golfer, she was one of the finest woman athletes of the twentieth century.

Orson Welles (1915–1985): An innovative filmmaker and actor, he directed and starred in *Citizen Kane,* a 1941 film that changed cinematic history.

Walt Whitman (1819–1892): A poet who broke with tradition, Whitman wrote *Leaves of Grass,* which he revised throughout his life.

Frank Capra (1897–1991): Famed in the motion-picture world, Capra directed *It Happened One Night, Mr. Smith Goes to Washington,* and the Christmas classic, *It's a Wonderful Life.*

Samuel F. B. Morse (1791–1872): Best known for inventing the telegraph and Morse code, he was also an accomplished painter.

Alexander Graham Bell (1847–1922): A teacher of the deaf, Bell invented the telephone.

Albert Einstein (1879–1955): One of the greatest scientists of all time, Einstein developed the theory of relativity, which revolutionized thinking about space and time.

Roberto Clemente (1934–1972): Outfielder for the Pittsburgh Pirates and the first Latino baseball player elected to the Baseball Hall of Fame, Clemente was dedicated to helping others. He died in a plane crash as he traveled to Nicaragua to aid victims of an earthquake.

Walt Disney (1901–1966): A cartoonist, filmmaker, and entrepreneur, he founded the company that has given us much-loved characters like Mickey Mouse, Donald Duck, and Goofy. He won a record twenty-six Academy Awards.

Jackson Pollock (1912–1956): An artist who influenced many others, he created large-scale abstract paintings by pouring or spattering paint instead of using a brush.

John Glenn (1921–): In 1962 Glenn became the first American to orbit the earth. In 1998, during his fourth and last term in the U.S. Senate, he became the oldest person to go into space.

Mark Twain (1835–1910): An author whose real name was Samuel Langhorne Clemens, Twain wrote *The Adventures of Huckleberry Finn* and "The Celebrated Jumping Frog of Calaveras County," among many other works.

George Washington Carver (1864–1943): An agricultural researcher, Carver developed hundreds of uses for peanuts. His insights about crop rotation changed the agricultural practices of Southern farmers.

Amelia Earhart (1897–1937): A pilot, she was the first woman to fly solo across the Atlantic as well as the first woman to fly solo across the Pacific. While she was attempting an around-the-world flight, her airplane disappeared. It was never found.

George Balanchine (1904–1983): One of ballet's most important choreographers, he created more than two hundred dance works.

Under his artistic leadership the New York City Ballet became one of the outstanding dance companies in the world.

Helen Keller (1880–1968): Although a childhood illness left her both blind and deaf, she became an author, lecturer, and social activist.

Yo-Yo Ma (1955–): A world-renowned cellist, he performs as a soloist and has played with other noted American musicians, such as violinist Pinchas Zukerman and pianist Emanuel Ax.

Louise Nevelson (1900–1988): The first important woman sculptor of the twentieth century, Nevelson assembled strikingly designed vertical boxes into dramatic wall sculptures.

Mark Hopkins (1802–1887): Hopkins was a college president and teacher of legendary skill. One of his pupils, James A. Garfield, who became the twentieth president of the United States, declared that "the ideal college is Mark Hopkins on one end of a log and a student on the other."

Mary Cassatt (1844–1926): An American impressionist painter, she is particularly remembered for her perceptive portraits of women and children.

Neil Armstrong (1930–): The first man on the moon, astronaut Armstrong left behind a plaque that reads: "Here men from the planet earth first set foot upon the moon, July 1969, A.D. We came in peace for all mankind."

John James Audubon (1785–1851): An artist and student of nature, he depicted more than a thousand birds in his work *The Birds of America*.

Luis Alvarez (1911–1988): A physicist, he was awarded a Nobel Prize in Physics in 1968 for his work in high-energy physics.

Richard Rodgers (1902–1979) and Oscar Hammerstein II (1895–1960): A composer and a lyricist, they teamed to create such outstanding musicals as *Carousel, Oklahoma!, The Sound of Music,* and *The King and* I.

Marian Anderson (1897–1993): After being denied permission to sing in Washington's Constitution Hall in 1939, Anderson thrilled a crowd that gathered to hear her at the Lincoln Memorial. In 1955 she became the first African-American to sing as a soloist as a member of New York's Metropolitan Opera Company.

Stephen Crane (1871–1900): A novelist and short-story writer, Crane authored remarkably realistic fiction. *The Red Badge of Courage* is his most famous work.

Ernest Hemingway (1899–1961): An avid sportsman, he was one of America's most famous writers. His works include *The Sun Also Rises, A Farewell to Arms,* and *The Old Man and the Sea*.

Langston Hughes (1902–1967): A writer best known for his poetry, Hughes utilized the traditions of African-American culture in his work. His books include *Weary Blues* and *The Big Sea*.

Frank Lloyd Wright (1867–1959): One of the greatest twentieth-century architects, Wright insisted that his buildings be integrated with their natural surroundings.

Ansel Adams (1902–1984): America's foremost nature photographer, Adams captured the beauty and drama of the American West in his black-and-white photographs.

Scott Joplin (1868–1917): Known as "the king of ragtime," Joplin created such pieces as "The Entertainer" and "Maple Leaf Rag."

Willa Cather (1873–1947): One of the greatest American novelists, Cather wrote of the frontier experience in works such as *O Pioneers!* and *My Ántonia*.

John F. Kennedy talked about the importance of going to the moon at Rice University on September 12, 1962.

R
The first ten amendments to the Constitution, adopted in 1791, are known as the Bill of Rights. They are, in brief:

I. Freedom of religion, freedom of speech, freedom of the press, freedom of assembly
II. The right to bear arms
III. No soldiers billeted in private homes during peacetime
IV. No unreasonable search and seizure
V. The right not to be a witness against oneself
VI. The right to a speedy and public trial
VII. The right to trial by jury
VIII. No cruel or unusual punishment
IX. Rights set forth in Constitution not to be construed to deny others retained by the people
X. Powers not delegated to the United States by the Constitution reserved to the states or the people

The right to vote is protected by a number of amendments, including XV, XIX, XXIV, and XXVI.

S
Lucretia Mott (1793–1880): A Quaker antislavery advocate and an early women's rights activist, she joined with Elizabeth Cady Stanton to organize the first women's rights convention. It was held in Seneca Falls, New York, in 1848.

Lucy Stone (1818–1893): An abolitionist and widely traveled lecturer on woman suffrage, Stone was one of the first women's rights advocates to keep her maiden name after marrying.

Alice Paul (1885–1977): A militant in the struggle for women's rights, she picketed the White House to highlight the suffrage cause. When women got the vote, she began a lifelong struggle for an Equal Rights Amendment to the Constitution.

Susan B. Anthony (1820–1906): She dedicated her adult years to getting women the right to vote, and although she did not see success in her lifetime, she was confident in the outcome. "Failure is impossible!" she said shortly before her death.

Elizabeth Cady Stanton (1815–1902): She drafted the "Declaration of Sentiments," which declared that "men and women are created equal," for the Seneca Falls Convention in 1848 and for fifty years led the effort to get the vote for women.

Esther Hobart Morris (1814–1902): As Justice of the Peace in South Pass, Wyoming, in 1870, she was the first woman in America to hold judicial office. Wyoming Territory granted women voting rights in 1869, and when Wyoming entered the Union in 1890, it became the first state in which women had full suffrage.

Amelia Bloomer (1818–1894): A newspaper publisher and editor, she was an advocate of dress reform. When she published a picture of the outfit some suffragists favored (long pants under a knee-length skirt), the pants became known as "bloomers."

Carrie Chapman Catt (1859–1947): A leader of the second generation of suffragists, she fought tirelessly to win the vote for women.

Sojourner Truth (1797?–1883): After escaping slavery, she joined the abolitionist movement and was a champion of the rights of African Americans and women. When it was said that women were too weak to be full citizens, she recounted the hardships she had endured and asked, "Ain't I a woman?"

T and U

The border of these pages pays tribute to holidays that are important to different groups in this country as well as to holidays like Presidents' Day, Martin Luther King Jr. Day, Labor Day, and Veterans Day that we recognize as a nation.

E pluribus unum is a Latin phrase meaning "out of many, one." It appears on the Great Seal of the United States, and today symbolizes one nation encompassing people of many different races, religions, and national origins.

V

Alvin C. York and Audie Murphy, as well as those named in the border, are some of the thousands of Americans who have been awarded the Congressional Medal of Honor since 1863, when it was first presented. Given personally by the president of the United States, the medal is the nation's highest decoration and recognizes "individual gallantry at the risk of life above and beyond the call of duty." Accounts of the valorous service of Medal of Honor recipients can be found on the Web site of the Congressional Medal of Honor Society: www.cmohs.org.

W

Washington was born in Virginia in 1732. He led American forces from 1775 to 1783. President from 1789 to 1797, he wrote, "I walk on untrodden ground," in a January 9, 1790, letter to Catherine Macaulay Graham less than a year after assuming office.

During Washington's time, it was popular to toast him as "the man who unites all hearts."

Washington died in 1799. "First in war, first in peace, and first in the hearts of his countrymen" was part of a tribute to him composed after his death by Henry Lee, a Virginia congressman who had known Washington for many years.

X

The clash of British troops and American minutemen at Lexington and Concord in April 1775 was an earthshaking event. Ralph Waldo Emerson commemorated it with the poem, "Concord Hymn," which begins, "By the rude bridge that arched the flood, / Their flag to April's breeze unfurled, / Here once the embattled farmers stood / And fired the shot heard round the world."

When British troops under the command of Lord Cornwallis surrendered to Americans under the command of General Washington at Yorktown on October 19, 1781, the war was effectively over. The Treaty of Paris, which formally ended the war and recognized American independence, was signed on September 3, 1783.

Congress approved the Potomac location of the nation's capital in 1790, but it was ten years before our national government was officially located there. Meanwhile the capital moved from New York, where George Washington was sworn in, to Philadelphia. In 1800 Washington, D.C., became the seat of national government.

Y

Benjamin Franklin gave this advice in the 1737 edition of *Poor Richard's Almanac*.

Z

The quotation from Ronald Reagan is contained in the 1994 letter he wrote to the nation saying that he had Alzheimer's disease: "I now begin the journey that will lead me into the sunset of my life. I know that for America there will always be a bright dawn ahead."

The opening pages of this book depict a celebration in New York harbor. The closing ones show a sunrise along the coast of California. The concluding words are the last lines of "America the Beautiful."